ON
AT

School Based Management
A Process for Change

Carl L. Marburger

The National Committee for Citizens in Education
is happy to record special appreciation to the
Spencer T. and Ann W. Olin Foundation
for its financial support and for
expressions of encouragement in
seeing this effort through
to completion.

Published by:

The National Committee for Citizens in Education
711 2nd St. N.E. Suite 100
Washington, D.C. 20002-4307
10840 Little Patuxent Parkway, Suite 301
Columbia, Maryland 21044-3104

Second Printing 1988, Third Printing 1989, Fourth Printing 1991

Cover Design by Bette Lucey

ISBN No. 0-934460-23-X PBK
Library of Congress Catalog Number 85-61225

Manufactured and printed in the United State of America

Table of Contents

Dedication v

Notes About the Author vii

Acknowledgments ix

Preface xi

Chapter 1. Decision Making in Public School Systems 1
- A Brief History 3
- Who Runs the Schools Today? 5
- Superintendent 6
- Local School Board 7
- Principal 8
- Teachers and Teacher Organizations 9
- Parents and Citizens 10
- Who Has the Most Power? 11

Chapter 2. Why Should Decision Making Be Decentralized? 15
- The Problems 17
- School Based Management: A Process .. 19
- Rationale for School Based Management 20

Chapter 3. What Is School Based Management? 23

Chapter 4. School Based Management Councils 33
- Membership 35
- Size 36
- Selection Process 37
- Selection of Community Members 39
- Relationship with the School Board 40

Relationship with the Superintendent ... 41
The Role of the Principal ... 45
A Memorandum of Agreement Between the Council and the Central Office ... 47
What Can School Councils Do? ... 48
Training ... 54
Meeting Musts ... 56

Chapter 5. How to Get Started ... 59
The Superintendent ... 61
State Mandated Programs ... 63
Other External Forces ... 64
Other Internal Forces ... 65
Problems and Hazards ... 67

Chapter 6. Conclusion ... 71

Notes ... 75

Bibliography ... 77

Dedication

To Stephanie, for being
what granddaughters are supposed to be.

Notes About the Author

Carl Marburger is one of three Senior Associates responsible to a Board of Directors for the operation of the National Committee for Citizens in Education (NCCE). He is a parent, and has been a public school teacher and administrator. Prior to coming to NCCE he was Commissioner of Education for the State of New Jersey.

He has been responsible for the school based management training conducted by NCCE and convened the first symposium on SBM in Denver in 1978. Long a practitioner of democratic decision making, he brings a passion and enthusiasm to this process called school based management.

Acknowledgments

This is always a difficult task for me. I am the product of all the loving, caring, and nurturing of so many, and I hereby acknowledge all those who have touched my life and who have helped create who I am. This is a difficult task also because I am no longer sure about the sequence of events that led me to my passion for school based management and the sharing of decisions with all those affected by those decisions.

To my many American Indian friends, I express my gratitude for reinforcing my beliefs in sharing decisions.

To Shelly Weinstein and Doug Mitchell who worked with me on the Commission on Educational Governance, my gratitude for clarifying the concept of decentralization of decision making, which led to my understanding of the school based management concept.

To Barbara Thain McNeel, who has made our SBM training experience both joyful and incredibly productive, and who brings a vast array of skills, talents, and humanity to whatever she undertakes, my appreciation.

To Phyllis Clay I owe much. As the director of the National Committee's training program, she showed me the importance of careful and meticulous design work, and together we began the basic conceptualization of the SBM training program.

To Judy Vogel, Wes Morgan, and Bess Howard, I express my gratitude for the opportunities we had to work and train together.

I am also most grateful to the school based councils consisting of principals, teachers, and parents in the pilot SBM school districts in New Jersey. Pine Hill, South Brunswick, and Vernon Township were the first of the pilot schools and their training was supported by a gift from an anonymous Rockefeller family member. That same contributor also enabled NCCE to work with school councils in Galloway Township and Perth Amboy, New Jersey.

Melanie Barron of the Boston public schools also provided me with an opportunity to work with her and to test some school based management concepts in the Boston public schools.

To Jerome Jones, superintendent of schools in St. Louis, Missouri, I express my gratitude for allowing us to begin the SBM process in the entire school system. That is an act of faith.

M. Donald Thomas, the former superintendent of schools in Salt Lake City, Utah, has been an inspiration to me since I have known him. Don is a man of courage and conviction and a true believer in the shared governance concept. And to Don, I express my gratitude for his diligence in reading the manuscript and for his insightful comments. The same could be said for all those who took the time to read the manuscript and to share their thoughtful suggestions. So to Cathy Hilton, Barbara Feldt, John McAdams, Stephanie Craib, and NCCE board member, Barbara O. Taylor, I say a very special thanks.

To my colleagues, Chrissie Bamber, Nancy Berla, Anne Henderson, Bill Rioux, and Stan Salett, I owe so very much. They have encouraged me to continue this effort when things looked bleak, they have "nagged" me to meet deadlines, and they have trusted and cared for me.

Lynn Holmes, Pat Fort, Maryanne Blair, Beverly Norbeck, Jackie Mosberg, Joanne Vaccaro, and Janet Gosnell have typed, proofread, teased, and encouraged me, and I am most grateful to them all.

To the Board of the National Committee and to Laurie Auchincloss especially, I give special thanks for their support of the concept and their encouragement in pursuing this handbook.

I save my most special gratitude to Barbara J. Hansen. Her dissertation says so many things I wanted to say so much better, so with her permission and with appropriate notations, I have used sections of her work intact. Most of all, however, I truly value her love and trust and caring, and I thank her for allowing me to be who I am.

Preface

School based management (SBM) is a new approach being tried in a number of states and local school systems, in which decisions that have traditionally been made by a superintendent or school board are now being made by the local school. It's a decentralized form of organization, in which decisions are made by those who know and care most about the quality of the education students receive—the principal, teachers, parents and citizens, and the students themselves.

This material is intended for those who would like to know more about school based management and who might be inspired to try to begin the process in their local school or school district. By the time you read this, it will have been through many readings by principals, teachers, parents, and citizens in order to assure its readability and its freedom from standard education gobbledygook.

We hope that superintendents will read this and begin to explore SBM with central office staff, principals, and the board of education. We hope they will realize that sharing power with others increases their own power.

We hope that school board members will read this, become enamored of the school based management concept, and encourage the superintendent to provide them with further information and guidance about how to initiate it in their school district.

We also hope that parents and citizens who read this will recognize SBM as an effective way to become more involved in decisions being made at their child's school building as opposed to those at a district level.

And for those students who may be involved in SBM councils in their schools, we hope they see in SBM an opportunity to be truly involved in important decisions that affect their schooling and perhaps even the rest of their lives.

For all of you who read this and who become involved in

some form of school based management, we hope that you take away this central notion of what SBM is about. SBM is a process, *not* a product! SBM is a *trust* process. That means that the superintendent and the board of education trust the local school principal to involve her or his faculty, students, parents, and community in the decision making processes at the local school and will share some of their authority with that principal. SBM also means that the principal, the teachers, the students, and the parents place enough trust in each other to join in making decisions that will be in the best interest of all the students at their school. If we do not operate from trust, then we operate from fear, and SBM can only function in a trust environment.

The National Committee has been involved with SBM since 1978, when with financial assistance from the Mott Foundation, we convened the first national conference on SBM. The conference, which took place in Denver, Colorado, explored the implications of SBM with practitioners, scholars, parents, and representatives from most of the professional education organizations. We also commissioned a state-of-the-art paper on SBM by Lawrence Pierce of the University of Oregon.

The NCCE then began a series of training events with six New Jersey school districts* and provided them with regular consultant and facilitation service for nearly three years. It is primarily that experience that enables us to write this handbook.

In addition, Carl Marburger, NCCE senior associate and author of this handbook, has spoken about SBM to hundreds of professional and lay groups around the country and has conducted many workshops on SBM for school councils.

SBM, if properly understood and appropriately implemented, can make a considerable contribution to improv-

---

*Pine Hill, South Brunswick, Vernon Township, Perth Amboy, Galloway Township, and for a shorter period, East Windsor.

ing our schools. It is our hope that this handbook will help in that effort, first by examining the centralized way school districts are now organized, then by showing a decentralized, school based management process can improve the quality of education at individual schools.

CHAPTER 1
Decision Making in Public School Systems

A Brief History

Who Runs the Schools Today?

Superintendent

Local School Board

Principal

Teachers and Teacher Organizations

Parents and Citizens

Who Has the Most Power?

There is a great similarity among school districts throughout the country. Most of them have a superintendent of schools, a lay body generally called a school board or school committee, and principals and teachers; they all have curriculum and organization structures that are amazingly alike. Most have established a bureaucracy to deal with ongoing problems and to keep things running smoothly. Most have developed a chain of command in which the superintendent and central office staff determine the necessary actions, and the local school staffs are expected to carry them out. Proponents of this centralized form of governance, where decisions are made at the central office, maintain that it is more efficient than when the district is decentralized.

A Brief History

Centralized decision making has not always been common in this country. Local or lay control of schools was indeed a reality prior to 1900. Each school had its own board of education with responsibility for all the maintenance, buildings, and ordering of supplies and books, in addition to the hiring and firing of teachers and general policy determination about what was to be taught. As school systems grew larger and the numbers of local boards increased, school districts were created, usually by state mandate, and district boards of education became the primary unit of management.

Around 1900, people called for "depoliticizing" schools

because of widespread corruption. Richard Hofstadter characterized this issue in the following statement:

> The urban boss, a dealer in public privileges who could command public support, became a more powerful figure. With him came that train of evils which so much preoccupied the liberal muckraking mind: the bartering of franchises, the building of tight urban political machines, the marshalling of hundreds of thousands of ignorant voters, the exacerbation of poverty and slums, the absence or excessive cost of municipal services, the cooperation between politics and "commercialized vice"—in short, the entire system of underground government and squalor.... [1]

Education was no exception to the corruption of the time. The schools, especially the city schools, were governed by ward bosses, and teachers frequently owed their jobs to these politicians. Contracts were let to relatives, and there was a substantial rate of kickback and bribery.

Public response to actual and perceived corruption was to create apolitical (nonpartisan) boards of education, to demand "more efficient" schools, and to hire professional managers for the school systems and the schools.

With the advent of the professional educator, and in line with the drive for more efficient operations, the nation's school systems adopted an industrial model. Schools were perceived as factories, with students the products that came out at the end of the assembly line. "Top-down" management was a natural function of that model, and layers of managers were created to increase the efficiency of the system and to supervise all activities as a way to guarantee quality control of the end product.

Managers or superintendents became more and more powerful as they gained staff to do their bidding and as they controlled the flow of information in an ever more complex system. School boards, which once were the major policy determiners and often the administrators of the system, were now often beholden to this administrator for information and direction. The superintendent had the power to control the decisions of the school system through control of information.

A remarkable increase in the centralization of school systems and in the power of superintendents came about through "government by administration" during the Roosevelt administration. The creation of agencies and bureaus to deal with the problems of the Depression and unemployment necessitated a vast system of managers to initiate and operate those units. School systems became large bureaucracies run, for the most part, by persons of good will. The governance structure of schools was, like government and industry, top down, with little input from the clients of the system.

Who Runs the Schools Today?

Decision making in public schools has become more and more centralized over the years. Decisions that were once made by teachers have been assumed by principals, and the decision-making authority of principals has been severely limited by central office administrators. Superintendents and school boards complain that state authorities have reduced their role to rubber stamps for state and federal mandates. And the public, especially in large cities, has found its ability to influence school decisions virtually wiped out.

Paradoxically, despite centralization, schools and school systems have remained loosely structured organizations, with little control exercised between levels of the operation. This often leads to orders from "on high" being circumvented or ignored. The authority to make decisions has been centralized at higher and higher levels, but the implementation of those decisions is often disregarded by those charged with carrying them out, especially if they had no voice in determining the decisions in the first place.[2] Many educational reforms have failed and will continue to fail in such centralized systems.

Let us look now at the people who make the decisions in

most school systems. Who has the power?

Superintendent

This person is responsible for administering the *entire* system—business matters, personnel, school property, budgets, maintenance, and overall curriculum, among other things. Helping him or her are a wide variety of assistants, administrators all, whose titles end with the words superintendent, administrator, or chancellor, and begin with such words as deputy, executive deputy, associate, or assistant. Each of these, depending on the size of the system, has assistants to help administer a particular piece of the system.

Most systems do have local superintendents, and most of these superintendents are appointed by their system's board of education. They generally serve at the pleasure of the board, although usually with a contract that runs for a specified number of years.

Some school systems, in rural Georgia, for example, elect their superintendents; in some states—Maryland is one—the county superintendents have responsibility for all the schools in their counties and there are no local superintendents.

As far as we know, no one has ever counted up the total number of school system superintendents throughout the country. The American Association of School Administrators (AASA) has about 25,000 members, but that figure means relatively little since many superintendents are not members of the organization and many administrators who *are* members are *not* superintendents. The closest we can come to a figure representing superintendents alone is to base it on the number of school districts in the country. There are about 16,000 of these. So 12,000 to 15,000 seems a likely figure: it takes into account superintendents who serve an entire county, those who serve intermediate districts, and those who serve area education agencies.

Local School Board

Here, too, the names vary with the states. There are school boards and school trustees and, in Massachusetts, school committees. But whatever their names, these groups serve as the policy-making bodies for their school districts, whether these districts are made up of a single city, suburb, or rural community, or of an entire county, or (as in Hawaii) an entire state. Boards generally have anywhere from three to eleven members, usually unpaid. It is not their responsibility to administer the schools in their districts, but to pass resolutions establishing policies that have the strength of laws and that are carried out by the local superintendents and their staffs. For example, if a board decides that any student who needs a free lunch should have one, that decision becomes a policy. It is then up to the superintendent to figure out how to carry it into action by determining which federal or state programs apply, how need is to be decided, etc. It is, however, the board's responsibility to keep track of the lunch program to see that it is implemented properly. This is called *oversight.*

Other board policies apply more directly to learning. For example, a board might decide: "By the time a student leaves the 8th grade, he or she must be reading at the 5th grade level, or better"; or "New teachers must be supervised (visited in their classrooms) and evaluated three times a year."

Obviously, school board policies frequently deal with complex issues, which can be extremely difficult to implement. To ask the right questions and to make intelligent decisions, board members have to do a lot of homework and usually have to rely on administrators for their information. This often leads to a situation in which the administrator, rather than the board, is the actual author of the resolutions that establish policy.

Board members are usually chosen through nonpartisan elections, although some are appointed, either by the mayor or by a panel of judges. Both the elective and appointive systems have their strengths and weaknesses. The elective process is more democratic, but it demands an extremely well-informed electorate. And although some appointees truly have the interests of students in mind, others are given their jobs for purely partisan or patronage reasons.

School boards, too, have their organizations, both at the state and national levels. The National School Boards Association (NSBA) in Washington, DC, represents boards in around 16,000 school districts. Since there are about 100,000 school board members in the 16,000 school districts across the country, these organizations have the potential of being a powerful influence in public education.

Principal

The principal is usually responsible for administering *one* school building, although in a few places the principal is responsible for several buildings. Among the principal's concerns are the safety and protection of students and teachers, the maintenance of the building, and the instruction of the students. The principal reports, through a chain of command, to the system's superintendent and has little contact with the board of education. Nor does the principal usually play any role in such system-wide processes as collective bargaining.

The principal does, however, exercise considerable influence in the local school community. Even when closely supervised by the superintendent and the superintendent's staff, the principal is reasonably free to determine the educational climate in the school building, its openness to the community, and the quality of teaching that takes place there. It is for this reason that, from the point of view of parents and students, the principal is the single most influential person in a school community.

Principals, too, have their organizations—the National Association of Elementary School Principals (NAESP) and the National Association of Secondary School Principals (NASSP), which covers both junior high and high schools. In some places, these organizations have merged at the state level, often with the superintendents' groups, to form various kinds of coalitions. Generally, however, the organizations tend to remain separate and narrow in their interests and concerns.

Before school systems became so large and centralized, principals had considerable power. They made most of the critical decisions affecting the operation of their school. They were often autonomous and, for the most part, were not accountable to others. As the centralization process continued, however, principals had less and less control over the operations of their buildings. They became part of a long chain of command from the superintendent, through assistant superintendents, area superintendents, and business managers. They rarely have significant input into collective bargaining negotiations, are given a budget under which they must operate, often have little discretion in the selection of personnel, must go through formidable channels to obtain needed repairs, and may have curriculum dictated to them. The above is, of course, a worst-case picture and fortunately many districts provide opportunities for principals to share in important educational decisions.

Teachers and Teacher Organizations

There are approximately 2,000,000 public school teachers in the country. The majority of teachers belong to either the National Education Association (NEA) or the American Federation of Teachers (AFT). The NEA has active state chapters in every state and represents nearly 75 percent of the nation's teachers. The AFT is less active at the state level. It represents most of the remaining 25 percent of the teachers, with a heavy concentration in the nation's large cities.

The move from teacher professionalism to teacher unionism is a fairly recent development. By the mid 1960s, teachers had for too long been at the mercy of school boards and school administrators, so they began to turn their professional organizations into unions. The professionalization of school management had long before reduced the decision-making responsibility of teachers to that of making up lesson plans and dealing with the day-to-day problems of educating a classroom of youngsters, often far larger than was felt to be educationally sound. Poor salaries were a widespread and chronic problem. Even though tenure had been instituted in most places in response to the outrage against political machinations in school districts, it is still little wonder that unionization became an attractive option. Teachers now have to be taken into consideration in educational decision making, if not through direct labor negotiations, at least by weight of their influence on the political process.

The growth of teachers' organizations can also be seen as one of the forces that has strengthened the move toward greater centralization of school districts. Collective bargaining is done at the district level, and decisions that affect all the individual schools are negotiated as a central policy with no variations permitted. Teachers, through organization and through the collective bargaining process, are challenging the dominance of professional administrators. They want a share of the decision-making power that has been in the hands of the superintendent and the board of education.

Parents and Citizens

We speak of parents and citizens together because we believe that education is a matter of concern to all persons, whether or not they have children in the public schools. What happens in schools affects our whole society and so affects everyone concerned with the quality of life in this country. We believe that parents and citizens need to demonstrate their concern through active participation in the affairs of public schools.

The most effective way for them to do that is through organizations and there are, indeed, a number of parent/citizen groups in the country. These groups can be classified in several ways. One is the way they started: whether they were parent/citizen initiated; or initiated by the school or the school system; or initiated by the state or federal government, as for example, the groups originally mandated by Title I of the Elementary and Secondary Education Act (ESEA).

Groups also organize for special purposes or objectives—special education, bilingual education, education of the gifted—or in response to such local issues as busing, textbooks, or violence in the schools.

Parents and citizens can become involved in many ways. Consider the following:

A. School Support Activities
   1. Audience—attendance at school functions
   2. School Program Support—fund-raising activities, hall and field trip monitoring

B. Instructional Support Activities
   1. Home Tutor—teaching their own children at home
   2. School Volunteer—tutoring, clerical
   3. Co-learner—participation with school staff in workshop and training activities

C. Governance Activities
   1. Advisory—serving on committees, making recommendations to principal or superintendent
   2. Decision Making—sharing decisions about school policy and activities with teachers and principals

Who Has the Most Power?

If we were to examine who currently can most influence the activities of individuals and groups involved in and concerned about the public schools, who has access to the information, and who makes the decisions that most affect the schools, we could design an influence scale that would be accurate for most school systems.

Hersey, Blanchard, and Natemeyer define power as "influence potential" and they further suggest seven bases of power which might prove helpful in understanding a "power line" or influence scale for school systems.

1. Coercive Power—compliance is induced because one can punish or withhold rewards.
2. Connection Power—compliance is induced because of the significant "connections" inside or outside the organization. Followers do not want to incur the disfavor of the connection.
3. Expert Power—based on the fact that there is a degree of expertise, skill, or knowledge that is respected by the group.
4. Information Power—one has access to information that is perceived as being of value to the group.
5. Legitimate Power—based on the position held in the organization, i.e., one has the "right" to expect compliance.
6. Referent Power—based on personality traits. . . .
7. Reward Power—based on the ability to reward those who comply.[3]

GREATEST POWER

Superintendents	
	Teacher Organizations
School Boards	
	Principals
Teachers	
	Parents/Citizens
Students	

LEAST POWER

We have examined the reasons for centralization of educational decision making and the roles and functions of the various participants in that process. Our next chapter will present an approach being tried in a number of states and local school systems that is intended to return the authority for decision making to the local school. This approach has a number of names: school site management, school based management, school site budgeting, school site councils. In this handbook, we shall use the name *school based management* or SBM as our way of describing this approach to decentralized decision making and decentralized governance of schools.

CHAPTER 2
Why Should Decision Making Be Decentralized?

The Problems

School Based Management: A Process

Rationale for School Based Management

The Problems

In the 150 years since the beginning of the common school movement, dramatic changes have occurred in the way we educate our children. Most families send their children to schools rather than teach them at home, and the majority of those schools are public schools.

Most schools are located in districts that are much larger than those of earlier years. By and large, decisions about what will happen in the schools of a district are made by professional school managers rather than by the communities the schools serve. Those decisions, however, are constrained by the laws, rules, and regulations dictated by courts, federal and state governments, and the desires of powerful teachers' unions and professional education organizations.

From total parent control of public education, we have come to almost no parent involvement; from one-room schools we have grown to multi-school districts and sprawling educational campuses; from clear, simple goals we have moved to fuzzy-focused purpose.[4] It is clear that American public schools need to change.

The report of the National Commission on Excellence in Education, issued in the spring of 1983, was the first of a series of recent reports critical of public schooling in this country. The name given the commission's report, *A Nation at Risk: The Imperative for Educational Reform*, clearly indicates the high degree of concern the commission members have about our schools. In their "open letter to the American people," they bluntly state that "the educational foundations of our society are presently being eroded by a rising tide of mediocrity that threatens our very future as a nation and as a people. We have," they go on to say, "in effect, been committing an act of unthinking, unilateral educational disarmament."

What is there about our public schools that warrants such words from this commission, echoed in many other recent reports on the state of American schooling? The litany is long, and each report has its own lists of what is wrong and how to fix it. We too could come up with what we believe is wrong, but we do not believe that such a listing would be useful or productive. Instead, let us reflect on what seems to have caused this sense of ill-being about the public schools.

- There is a general lack of faith in big government and big institutions. There is a conviction that large organizations are incapable of being truly responsive to individuals. Try to reach the person in a large corporation or in a large school system who can answer a specific question about a problem. How many phone calls and/or transfers of phone calls does it take to find out, "What is my responsibility as a parent for my child's individualized education plan (IEP)?" or "Whom do I talk to about the district suspension policy?"
- There is a loss of faith that professionals know best and that they have the best interest of people at heart. Gallup polls indicate that many parents and citizens still believe in leaving education to the educators because they know best. Yet the spate of commission reports and the information we at the National Committee for Citizens in Education receive through our hot line and through the mail, tell us that many parents have lost faith in the way our public schools are run.
- The cost of schooling escalates in spite of the decrease in student population. People associate increasing

costs with bigness, and when parents and citizens lack faith in large institutions like the schools, they vote down millage and bond issues and support tax revolts like Proposition 13 in California. Bigness itself causes anxiety and mistrust.

- The schools are essentially a monopoly. Most parents cannot change schools as easily as they might change doctors, lawyers, or supermarkets. There are few options for most families if the schooling experience for their children is inadequate.

These, then, are some of the reasons for the widespread discontent about American public schools as reflected in the reports that have been published lately. If these complaints are legitimate, what can we do about them? We suggest here that the process called school based management is one way of dealing with that frustration and discontent.

School Based Management: A Process

School based management differs from the traditional way of running schools in that a number of policy and budgeting decisions are made at the school building level rather than by the school board or the central administration of the school district. This represents a unique opportunity for planning to be "bottom up," rather than the traditional "top down."

The other essential feature of true school based management is that *all* those involved with that local school will participate in making those decisions. While this alternative form of school governance provides the principal with increased responsibilities and authority, it also gives parents and teachers the right to participate in important school decisions.

Rationale for School Based Management

The first rationale for moving to school based management is that schools should respond directly to parents' demands. Children are the beneficiaries of education. When parents are disappointed in the quality or content of the education their children receive, they have the right to insist on change; they have a right to call for more accountability.

They should also have the right to participate in the planning and decision making that produce the outcomes of schooling. They can participate effectively, and are most likely to do so, if the planning and decision making take place in their local school buildings. With school based management, the school program becomes "ours" rather than "theirs."

As more control is given to the school and community, public confidence in the schools increases, problem identification and solution become more timely and accurate, and the needs of individual students are more likely to be met.

A second rationale for school based management is that principals and teachers should have more control over school operations, particularly the instructional programs, because they are in the best position to know about the unique learning needs of their students.

The principal has always had an important influence on the success of school operations. Under school based management, the principal has the expanded opportunity to provide educational leadership, technical assistance, and guidance to the management of the school.

Teachers also have a strengthened role. School based management allows them a greater voice in school programs and policies.

John Goodlad, noted educator, researcher and author of *A Place Called School,* makes a strong case for local school decision making. His plan for school reform calls for reconstructing American public education "school by school." As he sees it, the greatest hindrance to educational reform has been the failure to see the local school as a social system and the focal point for improvement. Central to any school improvement, he believes, is staff dialogue about issues and problems, participation in decisions, involvement in actions taken, and responsibility for evaluating results.

Perhaps the best rationale for establishing school based management comes from the Monroe County (Florida) School District's philosophy about why that district embraced SBM:

1) When persons who will be affected by decisions participate and share in making those decisions, better decisions are made.

2) When persons are involved in making decisions, they have more ownership and commitment to outcomes.

3) People who function closest to decisions that must be made and who are involved in operating as a result of those decisions are in the best position to help make decisions affecting that operation.

4) When decisions affecting a school center and the educational programs provided by that school center are made by the persons responsible for implementation and outcomes of the programs, the school can respond more effectively to the needs of its students and the community it serves.

5) If school centers and teachers are to be accountable for results, they should share in making decisions about how the school center will operate.[5]

CHAPTER 3

What Is School Based Management?

School based management attempts to place maximum educational planning and accountability, and management of personnel and material resources, in the individual school centers. Educational research indicates that (1) school centers appear to be the largest educational units in which meaningful change can be brought about, and that (2) school principals appear to be the key agents for effecting change in a school.

Another definition of school based management comes from Oran South, a consultant to the Monroe County, Florida, school system from a presentation he made for Broward County, Florida, in 1978.

> School based management is a form of *district* (and state) organization and management in which the school-community system is the *key unit* for educational change and improvement . . . .
>
> Basically, the design issue revolves around the degree of *political* and *administrative* change desired, as decentralization can be administrative and/or political.
>
> Administrative decentralization, in general, is marked by moving authority for certain functions to different parts of an organization, while retaining power centrally. Political decentralization involves changing the power distribution. While relinquishing power appears to be giving up total power, experience indicates that the total system gains in power, and those at the top can get more results.[6]

Most school districts are now centrally organized. Such school districts create a physical as well as a psychological distance between the central office and the local school. It is at that local school that parent/citizen concern exists and where the teachers and principal can demonstrate that they care. All else—board of education resolutions, administrative and budget decisions, state and federal programs and regulations—have only one purpose: to facilitate what happens at that individual school.

School based management is a decentralized form of organization in which the power and the decisions now made by the superintendent and school board are shared with those who know and care most about the excellence of the education students receive—the teachers, the principal, the parents and citizens, and the students at each local school.

> The most important contact between school personnel and families takes place not at the district level, but at the local school. Parents and students are more interested in their particular school than in the district, and consequently, they are more likely to become involved at that school. Furthermore, by dividing districts into school units, the opportunities for parent participation are increased, while the scope of education problems considered and the number of people involved at any one meeting are reduced. This makes it easier to respond to parent preferences . . . .
>
> Likewise, it increases the chance of any one parent to influence school policy. Finally, school based management gives those education professionals most familiar with a student's problems—the principal and teachers—greater responsibility for the education of children. Since the educational needs of children within a school and between schools are not always the same, the principal and teachers in a school are in the best position to respond to those differences.[7]

Unlike many educational reforms, school based management is a *process*, not a prescription. There is no right way to implement school based management because the central theory behind it is the belief that each district and each school within that district is unique. Yet all forms of school based management have one thing in common: they reorganize the school district's decision making structure so that a significant number of decisions that directly or indirectly affect the education of children are made at the level of the local school.

No one invented school based management. Rather, it seems to have emerged independently as a response to problems that resulted from the centralization of decision making and a shift in society's values away from control and toward autonomy. The idiosyncratic nature of school based management makes it difficult to describe in definitive terms. School based management means both the delegation of some important decision-making authority to the local school and a restructuring of the way decisions are made.

Although it has been mentioned several times, it is important to restate who should be involved in the local school decision-making process. Most schools working with school based management use the mechanism of a school council. This body is called by many names: school site council, school improvement council, governance council, decision-making council, or school council. A complete description of the forms and functions of school site councils will be discussed at length in Chapter 4. Those persons who participate on the council are the principal, teachers, parents and community members, students, and support personnel. Not all of these participate on all councils, but it is essential that at least the principal, teachers, and parents be involved.

As the person held responsible for what happens at the local school, the principal must obviously be involved. The principal, who has often been called the most important single individual in the school community, is the instructional leader and the person secure enough to share decision-making powers with the council. The principal also has trust in the competence of the staff, the educability of all children, and the wisdom of parents about their own children.

*The involvement of teachers in the decision-making process is supported by researchers like Robert Fox, who reports that teachers who feel they are influential in decisions are more innovative and more likely to share their ideas with other teachers. They also feel less alienated from the school than their colleagues who feel less influential. Fox also states that most teachers want more decision-making power. Edward Caputo, the principal of a school that operates under school based management, supports these findings with practical experience. He says:

> The traditional model (where all changes are determined by top administrators and passed down to schools and teachers) has brought increasingly rigid methods of administering which tend to stifle creativity and send our best teachers into other professional fields to escape the pressure of that structure. The team management aspect of school based management mandates that the staff confer. This releases individual and collective brain power. . . . Teachers need the support of a team-like atmosphere in order to tear the loneliness out of teaching.[8]

Teachers are not the only people interested in having a greater voice in educational decisions. Parents and citizens are deeply concerned about their schools and must be included in the decision-making process. A survey by the Institute for Responsive Education found that 85 percent of the citizens and educators surveyed think the amount of citizen participation in education is too little. Teachers

---

*The material from here to the end of Chapter III has been modified from an unpublished dissertation from Barbara J. Hansen, "School Transformation: a Trust Process" pp. 88-92.

agree. In a poll conducted in 1981 by the National Education Association, over 90 percent of teachers in all parts of the country and at all levels indicated that more home-school interaction would be desirable. And clearly parents and citizens are interested in becoming personally involved with their schools. Nationwide, in 1978, there were an estimated 1,250,000 parent/citizen members of more than 100,000 school councils.[9]

In spite of this interest, the actual influence of parents and citizens on educational decision making is small. Studies show that equal participation by parents/citizens and educators is rare. Local community groups are generally ineffective in influencing educational policy because they lack the information and experience necessary for confronting the educational establishment. In fact, some studies have shown that mechanisms established for participation are illusory, that they are really intended to strengthen professional control over the schools. It may be the awareness of powerlessness on the part of parents that accounts for the perception of educators that most parents are not interested in participating in school management. As an Australian report on school based management puts it:

> When it is considered that schools for so long have been "fortresses," actively discouraging parental involvement or trivializing it where it is allowed, the cause of the problem becomes apparent. Apathy is closely related to lack of power. Where parents are given more real power to influence important decisions they will be more interested in participating. . . .
>
> Parents and community members are the true clients of the school. Parents pay for the school either directly or indirectly and should therefore be entitled to participate effectively in its operation.[10]

Instead of blaming parents for their seeming lack of

interest (and ignoring the fact that a goodly number of parents/citizens *are* interested and involved with their schools), educators need to look at their own fears about public and parental involvement.

When responses of principals and educators were separated in the survey of citizens and educators by the National Education Association, cited above, 34 percent said that the amount of citizen participation in education was about right (as compared to the 85 percent combined educator/citizen survey population that indicated the degree to be too low). One survey respondent stated that citizen participation "stalls practice, inhibits decision making . . . and wastes many man hours."

Obviously, not all principals feel this way. There is, in fact, some evidence to indicate that younger administrators, women, blacks, and Hispanics are more open to parent/citizen involvement. However, even those principals who believe that parent involvement increases commitment to and support for the school are fearful that councils will be taken over by vocal, special interest groups and believe their teachers feel threatened by parent involvement. Some teachers are not enthusiastic about parent participation in curriculum development, instruction, or school governance. They would rather see parents involved in assisting their children with homework assignments or in tutoring their children, with ideas for doing so coming from the teachers.

Clearly, the resistance to parent/citizen involvement is strong enough to have built an invisible wall between home and school. This wall makes it difficult for parents to either express their concerns or to demonstrate their support for the school. The tragedy is that, in an effort to blunt criticism, the schools have closed themselves off from needed support. Not only is this harmful to the schools, but it has negative effects on students. Students who view their parents as supporting the school have higher self-esteem and more positive attitudes toward school.[11]

What is more, the fear that parent involvement will lead to increased criticism seems to be largely unfounded. Restored confidence in the schools was one of the results identified in the home/school partnership programs of twenty-four of America's largest cities.[12]

Students are the most important constituency of the schools, yet they have the least amount of influence on their education and the environment in which it takes place. Rarely are students asked their opinions about the governance of their schools, and rarer still are they given the opportunity to make determinations that affect their lives within those schools. Yet one report from Australia states that research consistently shows student achievement lower and alienation higher in schools perceived as having a high degree of bureaucracy and emphasizing hierarchical structures. But the strongest argument for including students in decision making is that it provides them an opportunity to learn how to be responsible members of a democratic society. As that same report from New South Wales, Australia, puts it:

> True democracy depends not only on having a democratic constitution, but on providing real opportunities for people to learn its meaning and use. If a main task of the school is to educate children to be responsible members of society, it is imperative that its internal functioning should reflect those very democratic principles that our society is founded upon.[13]

CHAPTER 4
School Based Management Councils

Membership

Size

Selection Process

Selection of Community Members

Relationship with the School Board

Relationship with the Superintendent

The Role of the Principal

A Memorandum of Agreement Between the Council and the Central Office

What Can School Councils Do?

Training

Meeting Musts

If school based management is to be more than an idea, —if it is a process that is to be tried—there must be a mechanism for its implementation. That mechanism is the school based management council. The council follows the democratic model of representative government. Because the school community is so broad, it would be impossible to involve everyone directly. The key concerns in forming SBM councils are the membership and size of the council, the selection process, and the SBM council's relationship with the school board and superintendent.

Membership

As was suggested in the last chapter, different groups can be represented on councils, and those marked with an asterisk are necessary if it is to be called an SBM council:

- The principal*
- Teacher representatives*
- Parent representatives*
- Community members: usually nonparents or parents of nonpublic school students, business people, shopkeepers, senior citizens
- Student representatives: usually selected from secondary school student councils, but many elementary students are also included
- Support staff representatives: secretarial, custodial, aides, crossing guards

Some school districts (Monroe County School District, Florida, for one) initiated their SBM activities with just the principal and teachers' representatives and used parents in an advisory capacity only. While we do not recommend that as the best way to proceed, the unique circumstances in the district—a history of antagonism to "demanding" parents or bad experiences with the use of parent aides in classrooms—may make that the best way to begin. The disadvantages are obvious: parents who are brought in at a later date may well feel that all of the major decisions have been made, and the existing council of principal and teachers may have built a strong feeling of belonging, which will leave the parents feeling excluded or lacking in any influence.

Size

Size is always a concern for those beginning SBM councils. There is no absolute formula, but we do have some suggestions to achieve representation of all the groups. The principal, four teachers, and four parents would make the smallest group we would suggest. If students or other groups are to be included, the council should probably be larger. We also suggest that the council not be larger than twenty-three, so that it can achieve consensus or arrive at a decision within a reasonable period of time, while guaranteeing that everyone is heard. Some states, like California, have mandated the size of councils. California requires an even number of members, and an equal number of school personnel and parents/students/ community members on their school community councils. They even suggest ways to accomplish the balance, shown on the following chart:

Council size	10	12	14	16	18	20	22	24
The principal	1	1	1	1	1	1	1	1
Teachers (a majority)	3	4	4-5	5-6	5-7	6-8	6-9	7-10
Other school personnel	1	1	1-2	1-2	1-3	1-3	1-4	1-4
Total school staff group	5	6	7	8	9	10	11	12
At elementary schools Parents (or other community members)	5	6	7	8	9	10	11	12
At secondary schools Parents		3		4		5		6
Pupils		3		4		5		6
Total parents or parent-pupil group		6		8		10		12

Adapted from *Network for School Improvement* guides, California Network for School Improvement, 9100 West Pico Blvd., Los Angeles, CA 90035, and reproduced in "How to Make the Best School Site Councils in the World."[14]

Selection Process

There are many ways that the membership of the SBM council can be selected. Here are some of the mechanisms that may be used. The method you select should be the one that is most comfortable for you, taking into consideration the specialness of your school and school district:

Teacher Selection Alternatives

1. Appointment by the principal
2. Appointment by some faculty representatives, like department heads, faculty council, union representatives, etc.
3. Self-selection—those faculty who express an interest in the concept and a willingness to participate
4. Election by the faculty

In our experience, the last two are the most representative methods of selection and generally mean that the participants are willing to be council members and will work for what is best for the school and the students. Appointment, especially by the principal, might result in accusations of favoritism, or the selection of those who are most acquiescent or most fearful of contradicting the principal.

Parent Selection Alternatives

1. Appointment by the principal
2. Appointment by members of an existing parent group or legally mandated council
3. Election by the parents or parent group
4. Election of a majority by the parents or parent group, with a percentage appointed by those elected or by some other mechanism

Again, the last two choices would be our preference. Number four is the way we would particularly recommend, since it is more democratic and gives the council the opportunity to redress any imbalances that might occur in racial, ethnic, or geographical selections in the elective process. Appointment by the principal has all the potential drawbacks that were mentioned about the appointment of teachers. The Salt Lake City (Utah) School District, however, uses number two quite successfully. The PTA president, the PTA vice president, and the principal each nominate one community person to serve as representative, and each of those nominated members then nominates one additional member.

One particular concern that has been expressed by many persons is how to represent existing parent/citizen groups. The Chapter 1 (formerly Title I) federal Parent Advisory Councils (PACs), state-mandated parent groups, and those dealing with the concerns of the parents of handicapped children are all examples of groups that may have been established for some period of time and who need to be represented on the SBM council. How those representatives are selected can be a delicate political problem. Again, the specialness of the school and the perceptions of those groups about their role and their special turf have to be considered carefully. Our recommendation is that it be done openly, with candor and trust, soliciting the advice and counsel of those groups regarding recommendations for membership on the council.

Selection of Community Members

It is important here for us to spell out the importance for citizens other than parents of children in the school to be represented on the council. The school is part of a larger community and the school can and should be the focus for many of the social, political, and human service activities of that community. Senior citizens can contribute significantly to the well-being and the ongoing program activities of the school. One only has to look at what the Fort Lauderdale schools have accomplished with the help of seniors to know how effective they can be. Local business people, local shopkeepers who serve the children and the families from the school, and representatives of labor are all persons who can contribute significantly to the deliberations of the school council. This is especially true, as it is for all participants, if they know they can really have a voice in decisions that affect the school and affect their businesses.

Involvement of citizens also serves the self-interest of the school people. People who feel they count and have a legitimate voice in what happens in the school will support the school and the school district on millage, bond, and budget votes and become effective advocates for the schools.

Occasionally, the involvement of community participants directly on SBM councils proves too difficult because of their numbers or the difficulty of making choices among many very qualified persons. Some schools have made such groups special advisors to the SBM council and have established effective ways to communicate their deliberations with those advisors. They are particularly careful to let the advisors know when some action has taken place as a direct result of their input.

Relationship with the School Board

In defining the relationship between the council and the school board, the responsibilities of the school council must be clearly differentiated from the responsibilities of the district's school board.

The district board is created by state law and board members take an oath of office, swearing to uphold the laws of the state. They cannot delegate that responsibility to anyone or any group.

The board has the overall responsibility for the operation of the school system, but they can and do delegate a great part of that responsibility to the superintendent and staff.

They have the *sole* responsibility for setting the education policy for the district and they cannot delegate that. They *can* and do delegate to others responsibility for implementing those policies. Some of those responsibilities can be delegated to local school principals and to school based management councils.

District school board members have the responsibility for the quality of the education of all students in their district. They, therefore, have the responsibility to monitor their administrators and to hold them accountable for the implementation of the policies that set forth the means of accomplishing the desired quality. They cannot delegate that responsibility.

They are also fiscally responsible to the taxpayers of their district and to the state. They cannot delegate fiscal responsibility. They can, however, delegate some budgetary discretion to the local school and to the councils.

So, it needs to be clear that SBM councils are not little school boards, and have no standing in the law, but can only be creations of the board and the board's willingness to share some of its operational responsibility with those councils. Local councils can be the eyes and ears of the school board members, helping them understand the unique characteristics of each school. They can demonstrate how each school must implement board policies in ways that are most effective for the students in that school and its surrounding community.

Relationship with the Superintendent

We dealt with the role and functions of the superintendent of schools in Chapter 1. When school based management is initiated in a school district, however, there is some alteration in how those roles and functions are carried out.

School based management will not become a reality in a school district without the whole-hearted support of the chief school officer. Integral to the process of school based management is the willingness to delegate responsibility to schools and school councils, a willingness to share authority. Not all persons in authority are willing to do that; in fact, that willingness is quite rare. Yet we are aware of an increasing number of superintendents who recognize that empowering others truly empowers them. Not only authority is shared: information, which is often called the currency of power, is shared. Accountability is shared, as is the credit for jobs well done.

This dramatically alters the traditional roles and functions of the district superintendent. The organization is less divided by rank, and decision-making power is shared more equally among colleagues. The superintendent is still the person held responsible by the board for the quality of education in the district. But under school based management, the superintendent is no longer the sole responsible person. Superintendents who have instituted school based management in their districts have something to say about sharing power and the freedom that results from that experience. M. Donald Thomas, past superintendent of the Salt Lake City (Utah) schools, says the following:

> The aim of the wise is to empower others to use power to help themselves. It is through the diffusion of power that one becomes influential and effective.

Charles M. Ivory, superintendent of the Pine Hill (New Jersey) public schools, made these comments:

> The implementation of school based management has not only provided citizens with an opportunity for participation in decision making, but has provided a means for our school district to begin effective education of the public. A real understanding of our needs, accomplishments, and the manner by which we make decisions is developing.

Once a superintendent has endorsed the principles of SBM and has received board of education concurrence as a policy determination, some critical activities must take place.

- The board and superintendent must set down in *writing* a clear statement of the role of the district board and the role of the school based councils.
- Clear parameters or guidelines must be established

setting the limits of the decisions that can be made by the councils.

We have found that broader rather than specific guidelines give more flexibility and latitude to the councils without infringing on the statutory prerogatives of the central board of education. The guidelines used by the Salt Lake City public schools are the best we have encountered. Each community council participates actively in the decision-making process for the school, while operating within the following framework:

- To recognize and observe board of education policy
- To abide by state and federal law and regulations
- To stay within budget limits
- To promote ethical practice

Thus, the councils have considerable freedom to make decisions in the best interest of their students and their school without infringing on the responsibilities of the board of education. The local council, for example, could not undertake collective bargaining or nullify aspects of a contract with the teacher's organization. They could not institute a new curriculum that was in opposition to a board policy or disregard state law with respect to the number of hours mandated for physical education. They could, however, negotiate with the board of education to try a new curriculum that was not on the board's approved list or a text or supplemental reader that had not been approved. That negotiation might result in a no, a yes, or "you have permission to try it on an experimental basis."

It has been our experience that boards of education have used school councils to test new policies. In one district where we have worked, the principals in the SBM schools asked for and received permission for the councils to have a role in interviewing all prospective teachers in the building. The past policy was that all teachers were assigned by the central office, and the local school had no voice in that selection. This process was tried experimentally, and the superintendent and board have indicated that they now wish to institute that procedure as district-wide policy.

Another critical aspect of council operations in the Salt Lake City system's written guidelines is: "Under the philosophy of shared governance . . . each school community council participates actively in the *decision-making process* for the school rather than in an *advisory capacity*" (emphasis added). This means that, if the decisions of the council are made within the parameters set by the board and superintendent, those decisions are not going to be vetoed by someone in higher authority. It means that no punitive action will be taken against a principal or a teacher because the decision made by the council is not entirely to the liking of the board or superintendent. It means that the board and the superintendent trust the school council to make decisions in the best interest of students and the community, and, in fact, recognize that they will probably make better decisions because they know best the uniqueness of their school.

Purely advisory committees can also be useful to boards and superintendents, but they are not decision making councils, and it is important to know the difference. Advisory councils can provide considerable expertise and advice on items of concern, and wise managers and policy setters take their recommendations very seriously and act upon them quickly. Not all managers and boards are so wise, and the advice of advisory committees can be and often is ignored. Occasionally, the advisory council serves some political purpose, and its recommendations can be safely placed on a shelf. In short, the success of advisory committees depends on the good will of the appointing authority.

The Role of the Principal

Managing a school is a difficult job. The principal is often faced with the conflicting demands of teachers and parents, must mediate between students and teachers, is caught between bureaucratic demands of central office staff and the needs of individual schools and, in addition, must handle all the necessary daily maintenance and operating functions while providing instructional leadership. There never seems to be enough time to do everything. And that is often a legitimate complaint, especially since the principal is held accountable for what happens in that school. Now, with school based management, we are suggesting a whole array of additional responsibilities and functions without additional assistance and with no immediate lessening of the responsibility or accountability.

There is no question that, particularly during the first year, there is an additional call on the time and energy of the principal. Our experience suggests, however, that as the council learns to do its work, the principal's load is considerably relieved. There is, of course, no relief from the accountability for the operation of the school and the learning that is supposed to take place. Thus, the principal will still be held responsible for the decisions that are made, even though in SBM those decisions are the shared decisions of the council with the principal as one member of that decision-making body. On some school councils, the principal, by his or her choice, is a member without vote, and has only an information-providing role.

It is quite legitimate for a principal to hold to him/herself some particular decisions. One principal made clear that he would not share decisions about placement of teachers in his building, and another wanted to retain the decisions related to student discipline. If the principal is open and clear about what decisions will be held at the time the council is formed, then those become the school council's parameters or guidelines. Too many decisions retained by the principal could be destructive to the operation of the council; most principals are sensitive to that and are careful to limit their powers in this area.

Participatory democracy is difficult. It is especially difficult to one who is accustomed to making all the decisions and seeing to it that others carry them out. The principal in a school based management school can no longer be the sole decider of what happens in that school. The principal is only a voice, albeit a strong voice because of the power of the position and the specialized training in management and/or curriculum. Ultimately, the principal of an SBM school has to trust the teachers, the community, and the students to make decisions that will be in the best interest of all the students and in the best interest of the school. The principal of an SBM school must be secure and confident about her/his leadership abilities and have confidence that the superintendent and school board trust him/her and the council.

This means that the agendas for council meetings should *not* be set by the principal, but by whatever structure the council establishes—president and principal, officers, etc. The principal, however, must have substantial input into the agenda, for she/he has the best overall understanding of the workings of the school and policy guidelines issued by the central office and the state.

The role of the principal with respect to veto of the council's decisions is another critical aspect of the SBM process. The principal might get away with an occasional veto, but if it happens very often or particularly on an issue in which the council strongly believes, the council will no longer trust the principal, will become less and less enthusiastic about its role, and will cease to function over time.

Thus, with the exception noted above, the decisions are made by the SBM council and are binding on all parties. The principal, who is a party to those decisions, is still accountable to the central office and must, therefore, trust implicitly the teachers, parents, and others who make up the council. I am often asked what a principal should do if a council decides to use the flexible supplies budget to buy only basketballs. If the principal has contributed her/his opinion and the consensus is still to buy only basketballs, the school buys basketballs. It would be an unusual circumstance that might dictate such a decision, and probably would never occur in real life, but if it did, that decision would need to be honored.

If that decision was about introducing a science program in grades one to three, the wisdom of the staff and the community representatives needs to be honored; although a principal might not totally agree, he/she is a member of the team that arrived at a consensus. If it is a true consensus, all members agree to work for the decision and agree not to sabotage it. This applies to the principal as well as to all other members of the council.

A Memorandum of Agreement Between the Council and the Central Office

In all of the situations in which we have worked, we felt that it was important to establish a memorandum of agreement between the council and the board of education and the superintendent. This provides a clarity of purpose and spells out the conditions and guidelines to which all can agree. Also, a record of the agreement of the parties is essential, in case of personnel change. Board of education members are often subject to election, teachers and principals are transferred or retired, and parents/citizens move. We include a section of such an agreement between the seven SBM pilot schools and the central office in the Boston public schools.

SECTION I: STATEMENT OF INTENT

WHEREAS the Boston Public Schools are committed to providing an effective and quality education to all students in a manner which provides equality of educational opportunity in appropriate educational settings, and

WHEREAS we believe the school building is the most appropriate place where decisions, planning, program implementation will result in increased accountability for improved educational outcomes,

NOW, THEREFORE, the parties agree to the following:

(SECTIONS II and III are statements by the central administration and the office of finance and administration, and the school based management and the pilot schools respectively, where each specify what they agree to do.)

We encourage each school district that undertakes some version of school based management to carefully design their own memorandum of agreement between themselves and the school council(s).

What Can School Councils Do?

Once the council is formed and the mission is clear to all the participants, some decisions need to be made about how to operate. Some councils wish to establish a set of bylaws to govern their activities. If that gives the members a sense of security, by all means set up a process, subcommittee or committee of the whole, to begin that formulation. By and large, that process can be a very tedious one and can occupy the energies of the council for a considerable period of time. If the council insists on bylaws, we recommend adapting an already-existing set and stating clearly the process for changing them.

A very important step for the council to take is to decide whether majority voting, unanimity or consensus will be the basis for making decisions. Asking for some help from human relations consultants in understanding the differences and the positive and negative aspects of each is an important first step.

The next step is for the council to determine what needs

to be done, and that is called a *needs assessment.* Some councils begin that process by constructing a questionnaire and asking for a response from teachers, administrators, community persons and, often, students. Other councils assess their schools by means of personal interviews and a sampling of teachers, community persons and, sometimes, students. We recommend the inclusion of students whenever possible, for they are often aware of problems that adults do not see. Regardless of the method used, determining the school's needs is a critical step. Only when the facts and data are available and the needs identified can the council proceed to the next step, which is the writing of a plan of action: "What do we do, now that we know what our needs are?"

A plan should contain some goals and measurable objectives. This, too, can be an arduous and painstaking task, especially for groups with little or no experience in writing goals and objectives. Here again, some help from the district office or outside consultants will speed the process. A plan should also deal with the classic questions: What? Who? and When? This simply means that each objective should state what the council wants to accomplish, by what time, and who will be responsible for doing it. Some statements are very lengthy and detailed, while others are brief and deal more in generalities than in specifics. The following are examples of stated plans of action:

- *By July of this year, the lunchroom committee will have tabulated the results of our poll of student attitudes about the school lunch program and will forward the results and our recommendations to the council for action.*
- *The faculty will set up the criteria for textbook selection by this April for review by the parent teacher organization steering committee.*
- *By June 1986, all students will be expected to have completed 40 hours of computer instruction.*

In their excellent research report, "Can Schools Reform Themselves? A Study of School-Based Improvement Programs," Jane David and Susan Peterson, of the Bay Area Research Group, reported the school councils they investigated used basically the same approaches to proceeding as planning bodies. All schools began by assessing their needs and writing a plan that targeted needs and proposed solutions, and then specified activities for carrying out the plan. All built in some accountability and monitoring of progress activities.

It is instructive to call upon David and Peterson's research to examine what they discovered about the content of the agendas in the planning process. They found that the schools in their sample typically dealt with noninstructional rather than instructional issues:

> Planning groups typically develop agendas that focus on noninstructional aspects of the school (e.g., discipline policies, community relations, physical plant improvements).... the central aim of these noninstructional efforts is usually to enhance the quality of life for the school's staff and clients. One reason for developing a noninstructional agenda is a belief that such changes are prerequisite to instructional improvement. Noninstructional agendas are particularly common in schools beset by behavior problems, absenteeism, and vandalism. In such schools, staff and parents do not expect much teaching and learning to occur; they have more immediate concerns about personal safety and standards for behavior.
>
> There are several other reasons for planning groups to gravitate toward noninstructional problems. One is that they tend to be viewed as collective problems—schoolwide issues which affect everyone and therefore require schoolwide solutions. Another is that groups find it comparatively easy to reach consensus on the definition of such problems (e.g., we have to get rid of drugs on the playground and get students into classrooms) and on proposed solutions (e.g., we need a new discipline code). Moreover, in the nonin-

> structional domain, teachers can specify solutions at an operational level. For example, a popular solution to discipline problems was to institute an "assertive discipline" policy which specifies what actions are to be taken in what situations.
>
> In the few schools we visited in which agendas focused on changes in instructional practices in the classroom, such content was inevitably the result of leadership from a change agent, the principal, or another staff member. The person exercising leadership had a vision of effective instructional practices* that applied across teachers and classrooms. The leader used the planning process as a vehicle for introducing teachers to his/her vision of effective instruction and elaborating this instructional agenda to fit the particulars of the school.[15]

Different schools and councils have organized their recommendations in different ways; you may find some of these to be helpful to your council. For instance, the Boston public school councils identified three categories of needs: instructional needs, management needs, and unique needs. The instructional category is self-explanatory. The management grouping includes items that are noninstructional, such as safety, lunchroom, discipline, the physical plant, community relations, marking systems, and budget and materials selection. Unique needs are those very special needs and concerns of a particular school. Bus traffic around the school was one unique concern for a school in St. Louis that had 23 buses serving their special needs students. Other unique needs expressed by some of the Boston project schools were:

- Develop a school climate that rewards positive behavior and meets the developmental needs of early adolescents. A few specific objectives were to reduce

---

*We thank Dan Duke for suggesting this phrase.

student suspension by 5 percent, to increase student performance by 5 percent, and to document the number of students who participate in extracurricular activities.

- Encourage relationships among agencies sharing the ________ school complex—the ________ Community School and the ________ Community Health Center.

John Lindelow makes a case for the establishment of goals in the three areas of budget, curriculum, and personnel. He states that alternative names for SBM, like school based budgeting and school site lump sum budgeting, give the clues to the importance of this item. The principals to whom we have talked, particularly in Monroe County, Florida, state quite frankly that it is control over major aspects of the budget that makes SBM possible in their schools.[16]

Budget. Many districts permit the principal to make the determinations with respect to the discretionary parts of the budget, like supplies and materials. This represents around 10 percent of the total budget, and if this is the only budget item that is available to the school, it makes a very good issue for the council's deliberations and decisions.

Many other districts make a "lump" sum available to the school, and the school (principal or the council) can make decisions about how to spend that money. As Lindelow points out, however, "Individual schools are not given the money outright. Instead, they purchase the services and products they need through or from the central office. The schools generate the decision to spend, and the central office carries out the schools' orders."[17]

This does not, however, relieve the central office of major monitoring and accountability responsibilities. For indeed, the board of education cannot turn over their statutory fiscal responsibility, although they can certainly delegate a major portion of that responsibility to the local schools.

All districts with whom we have worked placed some

restraints on the portion of the budget that is allocated to the schools. Certainly capital expenditures and expenses related to collective bargaining need to be kept centralized. Otherwise, the central office could turn a lump sum representing the majority of the budget over to a local school. Once district restraints have been defined, the central office would need to monitor whether state and federal law is being complied with, whether the district's educational goals and objectives are being met, and how well students are learning, in order to fulfill its major responsibilities.

Curriculum. In curriculum matters, such as the use of a particular reading program or a special emphasis on writing skills, the school should be the primary unit where the decisions are made. The central office generally defines what is to be learned and establishes broad goals for the schools to accomplish, but as long as the school accomplishes those goals it can be free to make decisions that are in the best interest of its children. The teachers, parents, and principal who know the uniqueness of their students and what their needs are should be able to make the best curriculum decisions. This is where the council, representing their constituencies, can be most effective: in making decisions about the best curriculum and materials for their students.

Personnel. In most school systems, the screening and placement of teachers is a central office function. Occasionally, principals or staff members will have some input in the selection of their school's teachers; in most cases, however, a teacher is simply assigned, and there is no choice in the matter. Central office personnel have a legitimate function in the screening of applicants for teaching in their system. They have a further responsibility to accommodate collective bargaining mandates and to guarantee compliance with civil rights laws. They do damage to their system, however, when they make the sole decisions about placement of teachers. A principal (or better yet, a council) needs to have some say about who is to join that school team. If difficult decisions are to be made affecting the curriculum, the budget, and the learning of the students in the school, the team must be able to work together without serious personnel problems. Planning and decision making is difficult enough; to have a staff person who is out of tune with the goals and objectives of the team and the community makes the task even more difficult.

Training

Most of the business of the councils—planning, evaluating, deciding—is done in meetings. The council might usually meet as a committee of the whole, but there will no doubt also be subcommittee meetings and meetings to be held with various constituencies. So, we make some assumptions about effective meetings. Effective meetings

- are planned—don't just happen;
- help build the group;
- encourage participation from all team members;
- enhance the credibility of the group and its leaders;
- are made more effective if the participants have an opportunity to undergo training in group processes together.

Effective meetings are more likely if the participants have had an opportunity to learn some of the basic principles of group dynamics or human relations training together in a workshop setting. Communicating to another person can be difficult. Communicating to a group of persons can be almost impossible, or at least frustrating and tension-producing. We each bring our egos, our stubbornness, our fears, our insecurities to each transaction with others. The fact that we do often make decisions that are effective seems remarkable in light of these very human obstructions that so often occur in groups.

Learning about how groups function and about your own behavior as a group member can facilitate the workings of a group and make meetings more effective. *We strongly recommend such training and do not introduce school based management to a school district without training the council members.*

This handbook is not intended to be a training manual, and we do not wish to load this section with the language of group dynamics. We do, however, wish to specify that some of the following goals are important in the training of council members:

- To achieve some clarity about how the group wishes to make decisions, and to clarify the distinction between majority-minority voting, consensus, and unanimity.
- To understand the distinction between the TASK functions, which get the job done, and the MAINTENANCE functions, which ensure smooth and effective teamwork within the group and describe the behaviors of members that facilitate or hinder the group activities.
- To understand that individuals, as part of a group, sequentially experience three basic needs: inclusion, control, and openness. This is a theory based on work by Will Schutz. One simplistic way to understand the terms is to describe them with these questions:

  Inclusion

  Am I in the group or out?
  Who else is in?
  Who else is out?

  Control

  Who is in charge?
  How can I influence others in the group?
  Who wins, who loses?

Openness

With whom do I feel close?
With whom do I feel distant?
Will I be able to live with the group?
Will the group be able to live with me?

- To understand the steps in systematic planning.
- To have some concept of leadership and power.

There are many other issues that come up in a training environment: how to deal with the nonparticipant, the person who has all the answers, or the one who dominates the meetings; how to give constructive feedback to each other; and how to make everyone feel comfortable. Role play, games, simulation, and other training techniques are useful in dealing with these issues.

Whether some or all of these are handled in training may not be as critical as the fact that the group is meeting together for an extended period of time and is beginning to trust one another and to reduce the level of tension and fear.

Meeting Musts

It should be obvious by now that being a member of a school based management council is a difficult job. We believe the rewards make the energy expenditure worthwhile.

One more topic should be included, however, before we move on to our next chapter. The following list of MEETING MUSTS will help any council have more effective meetings:

- Know why you, as a participant, are meeting
- Know who is there and why
- Have a chairperson
- Have an agenda

- Have clear expectations on time and "what you want to come away with" for the meeting as a whole as well as for each item
- Make sure that the people on the agenda and the chairperson know what they are asking the group to do and how much time they have
- Make people feel welcome so that they can "ease into" a meeting
- Clarify roles to be played in meetings, i.e., process observer, facilitator, secretary
- Structure the agenda according to the shape of the meeting—light beginning, light ending, and heavy middle
- Have the room set up in advance
- Know how you make decisions and follow the process
- Summarize throughout the meeting
- State next steps clearly
- Provide opportunity for exchange of ideas
- Start and end on time—or have a good reason for not doing so
- If possible, plan to hold some meetings "away" from the school

CHAPTER 5
How to Get Started

The Superintendent

State Mandated Programs

Other External Forces

Other Internal Forces

Problems and Hazards

The Superintendent

One of the most frequently asked questions about school based management is, "How do we get it started in our school or school district?" The answer is different for each situation, but in our experience, the superintendent is the key to initiating SBM, whether the effort is district wide, or in a school or schools within the district. Occasionally, principals can suggest that they would like to try SBM in their school, but without the endorsement of the superintendent, it would not be school based management. It could be shared decision making at the local school, where teachers, parents, and students have a real voice in the management of the school, but the superintendent could always object to the process and there would be no decentralization of the decisions made at the central office. While we encourage school principals to initiate local school decision making, without the superintendent's support and some budgetary flexibility, it would not be SBM and would not have the substantial impact on the learning of children that true SBM has demonstrated is possible.

It is also possible for a parent group to initiate school based management dialogue in a school or school system, as the Parents Union of Philadelphia did. They convened a conference on SBM and invited speakers from around the country to present ideas and evidence about the effectiveness of SBM to a group of parents and educators. They then set up a series of meetings with the new superintendent of schools and are now working on the possible implementation of SBM in some pilot schools. This is an unusual case. It takes a very strong and dedicated group of parents to initiate such activities.

So, the superintendent is key to the initiation and continuance of SBM in a school or school district. Two specific examples of that initiation might illuminate the point. Speaking to the principals and headmasters in the Boston public schools on August 25, 1981, Dr. Robert R. Spillane said, "We must decentralize some key decisions to the school building level and empower those who are closest to teachers and students and are most familiar with the issues." He concluded that the key factor in increasing school effectiveness is the building principal.

In the introduction to the training manual on shared governance for the Salt Lake public schools, the following statement is made:

> During the annual workshop for the Salt Lake Association of School Administrators, August 5, 1981, Dr. M. Donald Thomas, Superintendent of Schools, issued an ultimatum: school administrators would be able to understand and articulate the concept of shared governance to their constituents by the end of the 1981-82 school year. He went on to say that with the added pressures of an increasingly skeptical society upon the school districts of America, the shared governance system of district administration appears to be the most viable answer in the 1980s. Its importance, therefore, cannot be overemphasized.[18]

In our work with school districts and SBM, our initial contact has always been superintendents of schools. They have either expressed an interest in examining the concept or we have approached them with an invitation to have a school, schools, or the entire school district participate in SBM. In some cases, they have rejected the concept, did not feel that they or the district were ready, or were threatened by what they perceived as a loss of power. In those cases, SBM did not start in their districts.

State Mandated Programs

Occasionally, SBM can have its impetus from an external source. In three states, the legislatures have mandated some form of school based management or the formation of advisory or decision-making bodies at school sites.

In Florida, Governor Reuben Askew began the process by naming a citizens' committee in 1971 to recommend changes in the financing of the state's public schools. As a result of the recommendations of that committee, the legislature passed the Florida Education and Finance Program (FEFP), which had three purposes:

1. To equalize funding among districts and pupils
2. To decentralize most education decisions to the school building level
3. To increase citizen input in education decisions at the district and building level

This resulted in the creation of either school or district citizen advisory committees whose major function was to assist in the preparation of an annual report of progress for the school district. While no financial support was forthcoming at that time, in 1979 a law was passed that granted funds to local school committees. Each school district (in Florida, school districts are county districts) implemented SBM in its own way, and the success of its implementation depended on the leadership of the superintendent. Superintendent A.J. (Bookie) Henriquez of Monroe County (the Keys) and Superintendent James Longstreth of Alachua County were, among others, examples of chief school officials who took advantage of the legislation to institute SBM.

California was the second state to begin a form of SBM through legislative action. The predecessor legislation was the Early Childhood Education Program (ECE), which provided grants to individual schools. Advisory councils were formed to deal with the improvement of basic skills in kindergarten through grade three. This was followed five years later with the School Improvement Program (SIP) legislation, which provided resources from the state for forming a local school council with broad decision-making powers. The legislation spelled out the specific membership and clarified the decision-making roles and functions for those councils. The legislation created a funded partnership between the local schools and their communities.

One other state that has enacted legislation is South Carolina. In 1977, a combination of fiscal reform and new accountability mechanisms were enacted into a law that is called Defined Minimum Program (DMP); a part of the accountability aspect of the law called for the creation of school advisory councils in every school building. In 1984, councils became school improvement councils and were given greater authority to improve local schools!

Has mandating advisory councils, school improvement programs, or school site management worked? The evidence is becoming clear that the answer is yes, although some of the programs have not been in existence long enough to have definitive evidence that they have made a difference in the schooling experience of students.

Other External Forces

Foundations can also provide some financial resources that stimulate school districts to begin school based management activities. The National Committee for Citizens in Education began our research into SBM and conducted training in six school districts with help from a grant from the Mott Foundation. Subsequent grants for the training of school councils in New Jersey came from the Fund for New Jersey and the Charlotte Palmer Phillips Foundation, along with a contribution from an anonymous Rockefeller family member. In all of those cases, we were able to provide a small incentive to school districts who wished to consider initiating SBM in their district.

One of the most remarkable foundation efforts has been that of the Northwest Area Foundation of St. Paul, Minnesota, which awarded four grants to school districts in the Minneapolis-St. Paul area, one to Rochester, Minnesota, and one each in the states of Washington and Oregon. The total of $430,000 was to enable each school system to experiment with ways to move decision making from the district level to the individual school community. Each recipient "devised a pilot program in an individual school, which will meet to provide a voice for parents and other community residents as well as teachers, administrators and, in some instances, students."

Our (NCCE's) current efforts with the entire school system in St. Louis, Missouri, have been made possible by grants from the Danforth Foundation, and this handbook has been supported by the Spencer T. and Ann W. Olin Foundation of St. Louis, Missouri.

So, some foundations and corporate foundations have provided the resources and have, in some cases, been the catalysts for change in sponsoring SBM activities in many school districts.

Other external influences on starting SBM activities have been organizations like ours (NCCE), the Institute for Responsive Education (IRE) in Boston, and School Management Study Group (SMSG) in Salt Lake City, Utah. A few universities have also assisted in promoting SBM; for example, Harvard provided some support and the auspices for SBM activities in the Boston public schools.

Other Internal Forces

Certainly school boards can have a powerful influence on initiating or blocking the institution of SBM in their school districts. Even before Dr. Spillane became the superintendent of schools in Boston, Jean Sullivan McKeigue, who was president of the school committee, placed the SBM concept before the board as a policy issue, and school committee members have supported the efforts of the project. The same kind of support is what has made SBM possible in all the districts that have begun the process.

In one small school district with which we have worked, the school board not only supports the concept, but most effectively uses the school councils as their community outposts and for testing the sentiment of parents and citizens on proposed changes in structure and curriculum.

School boards, then, must do more than go along with the superintendent's proposal. They must support the concept and be willing to share some of the decisions they would normally make with the local school councils. They must also be willing signers of whatever contract is designed between the central office and the local school(s). Their continued support is vital to the success of an SBM program in their school system.

The principals themselves are also critical to the success of SBM. They rarely have an opportunity to initiate such a program, but they are key to what happens at that local school. We receive many requests for information about SBM from principals. We hear that they then present what they know to their superintendents, and SBM is often initiated in that district. The principal, however, who is unwilling to share decisions with faculty or with parents can block implementation of any SBM program initiated by the central office.

Teachers can also have a significant impact on the implementation of SBM, but, in our experience, have not been the initiators. Some state organizations have begun programs of change at the local school level involving local teachers and principals, but we have not heard of any who have involved parents in the process.

In summary, school based management can get started if the superintendents wish it to happen. The superintendent can be encouraged by principals and teachers, or by the community, or can be urged/ordered/directed by the school board. But the superintendent must be enthusiastic, or at a minimum supportive, about SBM if it is to have a chance to be implemented in the district. And the board of education must also endorse it as a policy matter for the district. Beyond that, it takes willing and, indeed, able principals, teachers, and parents to make it work.

Problems and Hazards

We might classify some of the problems that have occurred in the implementation of SBM in schools or in school districts by the origin of the problem, such as those emanating or created by the central office or the staff of a school, including the principal, and those stemming from the council activities.

The most common problems created by school districts:

- Failure to develop a comprehensive statement of commitment to the concept of SBM, including a purpose statement that specifies the roles and responsibilities of the superintendent and board, and of the principal and councils. These can often take the form of a contract between the parties.
- Inability to distinguish between and clarify the roles of the central board and the councils.
- Failure to distinguish the role of the council from the various mandated and permissive parent/citizen/teacher/student organizations already in existence in the district and in the schools. How does the council support or conflict with an existing parent group? How is the membership selected, and are representatives chosen from those groups? Is the Chapter 1 group recognized?
- Failure to provide training to the newly formed councils.

- Bureaucratic slowness in responding to the needs of councils.
- Failure to provide follow-up services, training, and facilitation help at council meetings.
- Failure to designate a person whose major responsibility is oversight of the SBM activities in the district.
- Drastic changes in the composition of the board and a reneging on the contract for SBM with the schools.
- Loss of a committed superintendent before the process has had time to become a part of the ongoing processes of the school and the system.
- Moving a principal to another school while the process is in its earliest stages.

The most common problems created by principals:

- Failure to enlist the support of most of the staff, including support personnel.
- Insistence on a veto power over the decisions of the council. If the principal is truly a member of the council, and most decisions are made by consensus of the council, it should be a rare occasion when the principal would need to veto a decision of the council.
- Always setting the agenda for the council meetings. Good leaders will always have their own agenda items, and will bring appropriate data to bear on the issues to be dealt with in the meetings. However, setting the agenda is best left to the chairperson of the council. The same applies to the principal who insists on taking or is cajoled into assuming the chair.

Problems created by councils:

- Giving the decision-making power to the principal.
- Taking on too complicated and difficult an issue as one of the first to be worked on.
- Failure to deal with the too-aggressive council member, and letting that person determine the course of the deliberations.
- Failing to establish norms or ground rules for how the

group is to behave. Are certain topics taboo, are we being overly polite to each other and always avoiding disagreement?
- Always looking to the principal for the answers.
- Failure to listen to each other and especially to parent or community members.

These are some of the pitfalls awaiting those who start SBM in their school district or school. No list of the problems can take into account all of the possible things that can go wrong. Most of the above can be resolved by effort and commitment to the concept, but those relating to the superintendent are most critical to the continued success of the process.

The possibility of problems, however, should not discourage parents from attempting to implement SBM in their school districts. Parents have an obligation to improve their schools and to do whatever is necessary to provide quality education for their children. Overcoming problems is part of the process to improve schools.

CHAPTER 6
Conclusion

The public schools of America are constantly being exhorted to change. Special interest groups often view the schools as their only vehicle for accomplishing their objectives. Politicians occasionally use the schools and/or teachers as scapegoats for personal gain. Reforms come and go like hula hoops, as new approaches to solving the incredible complexities of schooling and learning are devised.

These past few years have seen another wave of commission and committee reports, decrying the conditions of the schools and recommending a multitude of changes, which too often reflect anxiety about the country's economic position in the world or the fact that we may not be competitive with some other country. Without a great deal of research or understanding, we are prone to recommend adapting another country's approach to schooling, or "doing harder what they may be doing wrong."

One significant aspect of all of these recommendations and their resultant statutes or policy mandates is that they all are top-down hierarchies. They all originate at the state, with orders to school districts to implement policies. Or they begin with the federal government, with orders to the states or local school districts to obey, or face the consequences.

Regardless of the origin of the recommendation, the result of these actions is a top-down series of commands, often bureaucratically enforced, with a lot of paperwork and reports required. That system is based on fear. If you do not do "it," you will be [fired?—nobody really gets fired], [chastised], [devastated], [chewed out], [audited].

When reforms initiate from the bottom up, from the school to the district, from the community to the school, from the staff to the principal, we are involved in a process that is based on trust, not fear. That is what SBM is, and why it can be the means for reconstructing American education, ONE SCHOOL AT A TIME.

This is no panacea. It *is* a process, based on democratic principles, which has worked where it has been given a chance. It can work for you, too, if you give it that chance.

Notes

1. Quote from Guthrie, et al. "The Erosion of Lay Control." In National Committee for Citizens in Education Commission on Educational Governance publication, *Public Testimony on Public Schools.* Berkeley, CA: McCutchan Publishing Corporation, 1975, p. 94. Original quote from Hopstadter, Richard. *The Age of Reform.* New York: Vantage Books, 1955, p. 175.

2. This paragraph taken from Hansen, Barbara, "School Transformation: A Trust Process." International College, Los Angeles, CA. 1983, p. 85.

3. Modified from Hersey, Paul; Blanchard, Kenneth; and Watermeyer, Walter. *Schoolboard Leadership Perception, and the Impact of Power.* Center for Leadership Studies, La Jolla, CA, 1979.

4. Hansen, op. cit. pp. 24, 25.

5. Henriquez, Armando J. *School-Based Management.* Mimeographed, Monroe County School District, Key West, FL, January 1978, p. 1.

6. Taken from South, Oron. *School Based Management.* Unpublished outline of presentation for Breward County, Florida, August 1978.

7. Pierce, Lawrence C. "School Site Management," Occasional Paper of the Aspen Institute for Humanistic Studies: *Program for a Changing Society,* Palo Alto, CA, 1976, p.10.

8. Caputo, Edward M. "A Principal Reports: Brains=Heart = Courage=Managing on our Own: Six Years of School-Based Management in a Key Largo Elementary School." *Options in Learning,* New York Urban Coalition. As cited in Hansen, op. cit., p. 88.

9. Foster, Karen. "Elementary Principals' Attitudes Toward Parent/Citizen Involvement in Local School Decisionmaking: The Effect of Mandated School Councils." Unpublished dissertation proposal, The Catholic University of America, 1980. As cited in Hansen, op. cit., p. 89.

10. *The Case for School Based Decision Sharing.* NSW School Based Decision Making Project. New South Wales, Australia, 1978. As cited in Hansen, op. cit., pp. 89, 90, 92.

11. Fox, Robert S., et al. *Diagnosing Professional Climates of Schools.* Fairfax, VA: NTL Learning Resources Corporation, 1973. As cited in Hansen, op. cit., p. 91.

12. Moles, Oliver C. "Synthesis of Recent Research on Parent Participation in Children's Education." *Educational Leadership.* November 1982, 40 (2), 44-47. As cited in Hansen, op. cit., p. 91.

13. Modified from Hansen, op. cit., pp. 88-92.

14. Rosaler, Jean. "How to Make the Best School Site Councils in the World," a Guidebook for School Improvement Councils and Other School-Community groups. Published by the California State Department of Education, Sacramento, CA, 1979, p. 9.

15. David, Jane L. and Peterson, Susan M. "Can Schools Reform Themselves? A Study of School-Based Improvement Programs." Mimeographed, Bay Area Research Group, Palo Alto, CA, 1984, pp. 55-57.

16. Lindelow, John. "School Based Management," in Smith, Stuart C., Mazzarello, JoAnn, and Piele, Philip K., eds. *School Leadership, Handbook for Survival.* Eugene, OR: University of Oregon, ERIC Clearinghouse on Educational Management, 1981, p. 123.

17. Ibid.

18. Salt Lake City School District. "Shared Governance: Active Cooperation for a More Effective Education." Salt Lake City, Utah, 1983, p. 5.

Bibliography

American Association of School Administrators, "The Role of the Principal in Effective Schools: Problems & Solutions." *AASA Critical Issues Report*, AASA, Arlington, VA 1983.

Austin, Gilbert R. "Exemplary Schools and Their Identification," *New Directions for Testing and Measurement*, October 1981.

Boston Public Schools. "Goals for 1983-1984," *School Based Management*, Mimeographed.

Boston Public Schools. "Position Paper on SBM," *School Based Management*, Mimeographed, March 29, 1984.

Boston Public Schools. "School Based Management," Summer Institute, July 26 to August 6, 1982, Mimeographed.

Boston Public Schools. "School Based Management," Summer Institute, August 18, to 23, 1983, Mimeographed.

Caputo, Edward M. "A Principal Reports: Brains=Heart=Courage=Managing on Our Own: Six Years of School-Based Management in Key Largo Elementary School," *Options in Learning*, New York Urban Coalition.

California State Department of Education. "Establishing School Site Councils. California School Improvement Program." Sacramento, 1977.

Cervone, Barbara Tucker and O'Leary, Kathleen. "A Conceptual Framework for Parent Involvement." *Educational Leadership*. November 1982, *40*, (2), 48-49.

Clark, Terry A. "Introducing School Site Management: A Framework for Citizen Involvement." *A Handbook for Parents*, Published by Schoolwatch, Inc., Trenton, NJ, 1979.

Corcoran, Thomas B. and Hansen, Barbara J. "The Quest for Excellence." Trenton, NJ: New Jersey School Boards Association, 1983.

David, Jane L. and Peterson, Susan M. "Can Schools Reform Themselves? A Study of School-Based Improvement Programs." Mimeographed, Bay Area Research Group, Palo Alto, CA, 1984.

Foster, Karen. *Elementary Principals' Attitudes Toward Parent/ Citizen Involvement in Local School Decision Making: The Affect of Mandated School Councils.* Unpublished dissertation proposal, The Catholic University of America, 1980.

Gideonse, Hendrik; Holm, Duane: and Westheimer, Robert. *School Site Budgeting: Abstracting the Literature.* Education Panel of the Cincinatus Association, February 1981.

Gibb, Jack R. *Trust: A New View of Personal and Organizational Development.* Los Angeles, CA: The Guild of Tutors Press, 1978.

Gibboney, Richard. "School Site Management in the Philadelphia Public Schools." A Report to Chris Davis, Philadelphia Parents Union, Mimeographed, August 1982.

Goodlad, John I. *The Dynamics of Educational Change: Toward Responsive Schools.* New York: McGraw-Hill Book Co., 1975.

Goodlad, John I. *A Place Called School: Prospects for the Future.* New York: McGraw Hill Book Co., 1983.

Goodlad, John I. "What Some Schools and Classrooms Teach." *Educational Leadership,* April 1983, *40* (2), 8-19.

Greenhalgh, John. "School Site Budgeting." *The School Administrator,* Arlington, VA, December 1981, 1, 10-11.

Guthrie, James W.; Thomason, Diana K.; and Craig, Patricia A. "The Erosion of Lay Control," in National Committee for Citizens in Education Commission on Educational Governance: *Public Testimony on Public Schools.* Berkeley, CA: McCutchan Publishing Corporation, 1975.

Hansen, Barbara J. "School Transformation: A Trust Process," Unpublished Dissertation, International College, Los Angeles, CA, 1983.

Henderson, Anne. *Parent Participation—Student Achievement: The Evidence Grows.* National Committee for Citizens in Education, Columbia, MD, 1981.

Hersey, Paul; Blanchard, Kenneth; and Natemayer, Walter. *Situational Leadership, Perception, and the Impact of Power.* Center for Leadership Studies, La Jolla, CA, 1979.

Henriquez, Armando J. *School-Based Management.* Mimeographed, Monroe County School District, Key West, FL, January 1978.

Jenkins, Percy W. "Building Parent Participation in Urban Schools." *Principal,* National Association of Elementary School Principals, Arlington, VA, November 1981, 20-23.

Lezotte, Lawrence W. "Effective Schools Research and Implications." *Citizen Action in Education.* Institute for Responsive Education, Boston, MA, June 1982.

Lindelow, John. "School-Based Management." In Smith, Stuart C.; Mazzarella, JoAnn; and Piele, Philip K., eds. *School Leadership: Handbook for Survival.* Eugene, OR: University of Oregon, ERIC Clearinghouse on Educational Management, 1981.

Lyons, Peggy; Robbins, Al; and Smith, Allen; et al. "Involuntary Parents: A Handbook for Participation in Schools." Produced as part of a contract between the U.S. Education Department and System Development Corporation, Santa Monica, CA, 1982.

McCurdy, Jack. *The Role of the Principal in Effecting Schools: Problems and Solutions.* Produced by Education News Service for the American Association of School Administrators, Sacramento, CA 1983.

Miles, Warren R. "The School Site Politics of Education: A Review of the Literature," submitted to *Educational Administration Quarterly*, November 1980.

Miles, William R. "The School Site Politics of Education: A Review of the Literature." Unpublished paper, November 1980.

Moles, Oliver C. "Synthesis of Recent Research on Parent Participation in Children's Education." *Educational Leadership*, November 1982, *40* (2), 44-47.

National Commission on Excellence in Education. *A Nation at Risk: The Imperative for Educational Reform.* Washington, DC: April 1983.

National Urban Coalition. "Four Case Studies of School Site Lump Sum Budgeting." Preliminary draft, mimeographed. Washington, DC: National Urban Coalition (circa 1978).

Ornstein, Allan C. "Decentralization—Is It Working?" *Principal*, November 1981, *61*, 24.

Parker, Barbara. "School Based Management: Improve Education by Giving Parents, Principals More Control of Your Schools," *The American School Board Journal.* National School Boards Association, Alexandria, VA, Vol. 166, No. 7, July 1979, 20-24.

Pierce, Lawrence C. "School Based Management," *OSSC Bulletin*, Volume 23, Number 10. Oregon: Oregon School Study Council, University of Oregon, June 1980.

Pierce, Lawrence C. "School Based Management." Unpublished paper prepared for the National Committee for Citizens in Education, Columbia, MD, July 1978.

Pierce, Lawrence C. "School Site Management." Occasional

Paper of the Aspen Institute for Humanities Studies; Program for a Changing Society. Palo Alto, CA, 1976.

Pine Hill Public Schools. "School Based Management in the Pine Hill Schools—A Handbook for School Site Council Members." Pine Hill, NJ, Mimeographed, June 1983.

Reed, Donald B. and Mitchell, Douglas E. "The Structure of Citizen Participation: Public Decisions for Public Schools." *Public Testimony on Public Schools*, McCutchan Publishing Corporation, 1975.

Salt Lake City School District. "Shared Governance: Active Cooperation for a More Effective Education." Salt Lake City, Utah, 1983.

Salt Lake City Schools. "The School Community Council: Its Operation in the Salt Lake City Schools." Mimeographed, Salt Lake City, Utah.

Scriven, Michael. "A Procedure for Assessing the Performance of a Particular School," A Report to the San Francisco Public Schools Commission, Mimeographed, December 1976.

South, Oron. "School Based Management." Unpublished outline of presentation for Breward County, FL, August 1978.

Southeastern Public Education Program, Inc. "Parents Can Make a Difference—at School." *A SEPEP Report on Its School Needs Assessment Project.* Southeastern Public Education Program, Inc., Macon, GA, 1983.

Stallworth, John T. and William, David L., Jr. "A Survey of Parents Regarding Parent Involvement in the Schools." Mimeographed, Southwest Educational Development Laboratory, Austin, TX, 1982.

Task Force on Education for Economic Growth. *Action for Excellence: A Plan to Improve Our Nation's Schools.* Denver, CO: Education Commission of the States, 1983.

Taylor, Barbara Ann Olin. "Implementing What Works: Elementary Principals and School Improvement Programs." Unpublished dissertation, Northwestern University, 1984.

New South Wales School Based Decision Sharing Project. *The Case for School Based Decision Sharing.* New South Wales, Australia, 1978.

U.S. Department of Education, Office of Planning, Budget, and Evaluation. "The Study of Parental Involvement in Four Federal Education Programs." Executive Summary, Mimeographed, November 1982.